The Ultimate
JOURNAL TO FEEL
CONFIDENT, PRETTY, AND HAPPY

By Isabel & Emily Lluch
Age 16   Age 13

WS Publishing Group
www.WSPublishingGroup.com
San Diego, California 92119

The Ultimate Girls' Guide
JOURNAL TO FEEL
CONFIDENT, PRETTY, AND HAPPY

✿

BY ISABEL & EMILY LLUCH

Published by WS Publishing Group
San Diego, California 92119
Copyright © 2009 by WS Publishing Group

Nutritional and fitness guidelines based on information provided by the United States Food and
Drug Administration, Food and Nutrition Information Center, National Agricultural Library,
Agricultural Research Service, and the U.S. Department of Agriculture.

Designed by: David Defenbaugh & Sarah Jang, WS Publishing Group

For inquiries:
Log on to www.WSPublishingGroup.com
E-mail info@WSPublishingGroup.com

ISBN-13: 978-1-934386-59-0

Printed in China

Welcome to the Girls' Guide journal!

This book is fun, creative, and crazy – just like being a girl! Treat it like you would one of your best friends ... tell it everything that's on your mind. With tons of quizzes, charts, questions, and photo pages, this journal is your ultimate companion to being a girl.

This journal belongs to:

....

Date:

....

friends
family

Me

Place a favorite *photo* of you here.

☆ ☆ ☆

Your favorite quote:

Table of Contents

Warm-Up ✳

Getting Started . . .

Full name: ....

A name you would choose other than your own: ....

Your age: .... Birthday: ....

The weather today: ....

Something that made you happy today: ....

Something you are nervous about: ....

Something you are hopeful about: ....

The last person you called: ....

The last thing you ate: ....

The best thing about being a girl: ....

....

The worst thing about being a girl: ....

....

All About You

Your motto:...

....

Astrological sign: ....

Height:... Weight:...

Eye color:..................................... Shoe size: ....

Ethnicity:...

Siblings:...

Pets: ....

Three words to describe you:

....

....

....

Favorite number:...

Favorite color:...

Favorite celebrity: ....

Favorite food:..

Looking Your Best

Body Types

Every girl has a natural body type — rectangle, apple, pear, or hourglass. It's good to know which type you are so you can learn what exercises to do and the best ways to dress for your shape.

Which body type are you? ....

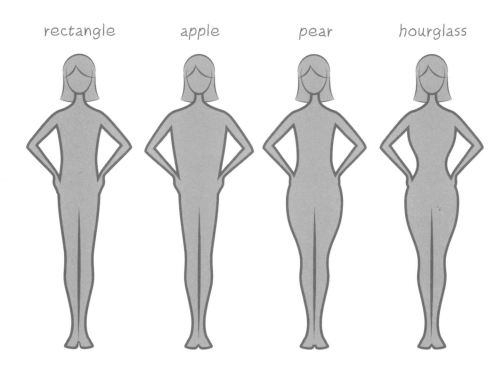

rectangle   apple   pear   hourglass

Your Body

What is your favorite thing about your body?..

....

Your least favorite thing?..

....

How has your body changed the most recently?...

....

....

What kinds of clothes are
the most flattering on you? ....

....

....

What is least flattering?..............................

....

....

Where do you tend to
gain the most weight? ....

....

❀ Looking Your Best ....

Celebrity Body

If you could have one celeb's body, whose would you choose?
Cut out a picture from a magazine and place it on this page.

What makes you
admire her figure?

....

....

....

....

....

....

....

....

....

....

Bikini Bliss

Do your parents let you wear bikinis?..

What is your biggest swimsuit frustration?.....................................

....

What is your favorite swimsuit style? ....

....

When was the last time you wore a swimsuit?...

....

Hair Type

Which words describe your hair type?
Check off the words that apply to you.

☐ Smooth   ☐ Curly   ☐ Oily

☐ Soft   ☐ Wiry   ☐ Dry

☐ Poofy   ☐ Thick   ☐ Shiny

☐ Flat   ☐ Split ends   ☐ Dull

☐ Frizzy   ☐ Thin   ☐ Wavy

Hair Dare!

Chemically straighten your hair, if your hair is curly, or get a Body Wave, if your hair is straight

No Way!

Cut bangs

No Way!

Totally

Totally

Start Here!

No Way!

Would you ...?
Wear pigtails to school

Get super-long extensions, à la Paris Hilton

No Way!

Totally

Totally

No Way!

Dye your hair platinum blonde

Get a pixie cut like Victoria Beckham

No Way!

Totally

Totally

No Way!

Get layers
all over

Turtle
– You're most comfortable with your own hairstyle, and you know what looks good on you. Just keep in mind it can't hurt to try something new once in a while, like cutting layers or getting highlights. The best part about hair is it always grows back.

Totally

No Way!

Dye your hair pink for a week

Totally

Butterfly – You
are open to change when it comes to your hair style. You aren't afraid to try a few styles and even colors. You know that experimenting with a new look can make you feel awesome and pretty!

No Way!

Shave your head for

$500

Chameleon
– You are confident enough to pull off any style, color or cut. You like to have fun with your hair, and you'll try any trend once. Girls wish they were as daring as you!

Totally

❀ Looking Your Best ....

Great Hair Day!

Place a *photo* of you having an
amazing hair day *here*.

What did you like about your hair on this occasion?...

....

What is your favorite way to wear your hair?...

....

Hair Idol

What celebrities have the best hairstyles?
Cut out pictures from magazines and place them here.

❀ Looking Your Best ....

Makeup Bag ✿ ✳

How do you feel about makeup?.............

....

....

Do you feel pressured to wear it?

....

Do you love it, hate it, feel better without it?..

....

....

When did you first start wearing makeup?..

....

Who taught you to use it?..

....

What makeup products can't you live without? ....

....

What makeup do you wear to school daily? ....

....

What do you wear when you're dressing up, like for a dance? ....

....

What is your favorite brand of makeup? ....

....

....

Is there a kind of makeup
you would like to learn to apply?

....

....

....

Warm or Cool?

Do you know if you have warm or cool skin tone? Choosing the right makeup shades and colors for your skin tone will mean looking bright and beautiful, so take the quiz below to find out if you are a Warm or Cool.

❶ When you're in the sun, do you turn pink or red or do you get a golden tan?

☐ Pink or red - Cool: Wear concealer and foundation with pink undertones

☐ Golden - Warm: Cover-up or foundation with yellow undertones is most flattering

❷ Do you have a natural glow in gold jewelry or does silver flatter you better?

☐ Gold - Warm: Try wearing eye shadow in earth tones like brown, gold, orange, and moss

☐ Silver - Cool: You'll look pretty in jewel-toned makeup, such as magenta, purple, silver, and blue

❸ How do you look in yellow clothing? Sunny and pretty or sallow and blotchy?

☐ Sunny - Warm: Brownish-black mascara will flatter your eyes

☐ Sallow - Cool: Jet-black mascara shows off your eyes

4 When you look at the inside of your wrist, what color are your veins? Blue or green?

☐ Blue - Cool: Ruby-red or bright pink lip color will look gorgeous on you

☐ Green - Warm: Experiment with lip glosses with subtle gold or copper shimmer

So which skin tone are you?

☐ **Warm**

☐ **Cool**

No matter what shape, size, and skin tone you are, you're beautiful!

❁ Looking Your Best ....

Flaunt It!

What is a feature you like to highlight with makeup? ....

....

What do you hide with makeup? ....

....

What is the one product that makes you feel the most beautiful? ....

....

What makeup product
would you never wear? ....

....

....

....

....

Hot Stuff

Place a *photo* of you in your
favorite outfit here.

What is your favorite outfit?..

How do you feel when you wear it?...

....

Why do you feel so good in this outfit?..

....

Hot or Not?

	Hot	Not
Sequins	❏	❏
Leather pants	❏	❏
Combat boots	❏	❏
Tutu	❏	❏
Thong	❏	❏
Fanny pack	❏	❏
Cowboy hat	❏	❏
Fur	❏	❏
Ankle boots	❏	❏
Colored tights	❏	❏
Leopard print	❏	❏

	Hot	Not
Tie-dye	❑	❑
Socks & sandals	❑	❑
Kimono	❑	❑
Monogramming	❑	❑
Scarf	❑	❑
Miniskirt	❑	❑
Cut-off shorts	❑	❑
Giant sunglasses	❑	❑
Leggings	❑	❑
Skinny jeans	❑	❑
UGG boots	❑	❑

Closet Covet

What are your most coveted fashion items? ....
....

CoLLaGE

Cut out pictures of your favorite shoes, accessories, bags, dresses, coats, and more, and create a collage of your fashion fantasy.

Fashion Frustration?

Do you feel pressured to wear designer labels or shop at special stores?

....

Do you ever feel bad because you can't afford a certain brand?.....................

....

Have you ever been made fun of for something you wore?.................................

....

Or is fitting in through fashion easy for you?..

....

Describe how fashion makes you feel.

....

....

....

....

....

....

Body Hygiene

Hygiene 101

How good is your hygiene?
Take this quiz and find out!

After a basketball game, you:

a. Say hi to your parents and head to the showers.

b. Spray on some perfume and meet friends for pizza.

You wash your face:

a. In the morning, before bed, and if you have a game.

b. If you're not too tired.

You floss:

a. Before bed, every night. Ugh ...

b. If you have something stuck in your teeth.

Deodorant is:

a. Easy to use and works!

b. For smelly girls.

You *have* to get glasses, so you:

    a. Shop around until you find a cute pair.

    b. Stash 'em in your backpack at school. You'd rather squint.

Your feet start to get smelly after gym class; you:

    a. Use baby powder in your shoes and wash your feet after class.

    b. Wear sneakers those days so know one will know.

How often do you wash your gym clothes?

    a. At least once a week.

    b. Whenever they start to stink up your locker.

Mostly a's: Having good hygiene and taking care of yourself is important to you, even though it's not always the most exciting part of your day. Keep it up and you will feel confident that you look (and smell) great.

Mostly b's: Hygiene isn't something to skimp on, even if things like flossing or washing your face take a little extra time. It will be worth it, we promise!

✿ Body Hygiene ....

Bathing Beauty

Buying a few good-smelling shower or bath products makes hygiene more fun. Plus, certain scents have relaxing or mood-boosting qualities! Put a check mark next to the scents you like.

☐ **Lavender:** Calming and relaxing, perfect for chilling out before bed

☐ **Oatmeal:** Good for soothing itchy or stressed-out skin, especially in the winter

☐ **Grapefruit or Tangerine:** Citrus scents perk you up and inspire creative juices to start flowing

☐ **Vanilla:** Vanilla, which smells homey and comforting, will amp up your mood and make you smile

☐ **Mint:** Perfect for an eye-opening shower before school when you're feeling sleepy

☐ **Coconut:** This yummy smell will make you think of an awesome tropical vacation

☐ **Lemon:** Lemon improves concentration, great before a big test

Everything You

Do you have braces?

❑ Yes

❑ No

Glasses are

❑ Cute

❑ Dorky

You prefer your nails

❑ Long

❑ Short

❑ Square

❑ Round

Your feet are

❑ Pretty

❑ Stinky

❑ All feet are gross!

In your ears you wear

❑ Small studs

❑ Long, dangly earrings

❑ Hoops

❑ I don't wear earrings!

Your eye color:

The eye color you would choose:

Your favorite color to paint your nails:

Skin Type

Choosing the right facial cleanser, lotion, and makeup for you means knowing your skin type.

Here's what to do:

1 Wash your face, pat it dry, and wait for at least an hour.

2 Then, press four different pieces of Kleenex to your nose, chin, cheeks, and forehead.

* If all four pieces of tissue are oily, you have **oily skin.**

* If you see dry flakes and no oil on the tissue, you have **dry skin.**

* If only the tissue from your forehead, chin and nose is oily, you have **combination skin,** meaning that your T-zone (the T that your forehead, chin and nose make) is oily but your cheeks are dry.

* If you don't see much oil or flakes at all, you have **normal skin!**

Your Skin Type:

....

Skin Stress!

Ugh, having oily or dry or zitty skin is so **frustrating!**

Talk about your biggest skin woes here.

How do you wish your skin was different? ....

....

....

....

....

What do you like about your skin? ....

....

....

....

....

....

Homemade Spa Day

Call up your girlfriends and have a spa day at your house. Give each other manicures and pedicures, mini-massages, and homemade facials using stuff that's right in your kitchen! Below are two easy recipes you can try.

Note: Just make sure you test each mixture on the back of your hand before spreading it all over your face or body so you know you're not allergic!

Banana Mash Facial
Mix half a mashed banana with 1 spoonful of honey and 2 spoonfuls of plain yogurt until smooth. Apply it to your face with your fingers and leave it on for 10 or 15 minutes. Wipe it off with a damp washcloth.

Notes:...   Review:
....   ☆　☆　☆　☆　☆
(Rate this facial!)

Sugar-Sweet Face & Body Scrub
Blend 1/4 cup honey, 3 spoonfuls of unsweetened cocoa powder, 2 spoonfuls olive oil, and 1/4 cup brown sugar to make a sweet face and body scrub. Blend it all over in small circles and rinse off in the shower. Voilà, smooth skin!

Notes:...   Review:
....   ☆　☆　☆　☆　☆
(Rate this facial!)

Place a *photo* of you during your homemade spa day here.

Write a review of your *homemade spa day*: ....
....
....
....
....

Signature Scent

Every girl should have her own signature scent. Look at the chart and find out which type of perfume fits your personality best.

Floral (rose, gardenia, jasmine, lavender)
You are a girlie girl who likes to look pretty and feminine. You tend to be a hopeless romantic.

Oriental (spices, vanilla, clove, orchid)
You are confident and passionate. You dress to be noticed and want an exotic scent that's perfect for dancing all night.

Fruity/Citrus (orange, grapefruit, apple, lemon)
You are fun and playful, with an optimistic and carefree attitude. Your friends would probably describe you as bubbly.

Woody (sandalwood, leather, cedar, moss)
You're a creative girl with a free spirit. You are an artist, poet, singer, or writer who loves to be out in nature.

Fresh (rain, grass, freesia, lotus)
You don't like anything super girlie. You prefer a natural, clean look that lets your confident personality show through.

Your Signature Scent: ....

On the Nose

I associate the following smells with:

Vanilla:...

Rain:..

Oranges: ....

Laundry:..

Fireplace:...

Barbecue: ....

Bread:..

Pine:..

Coffee: ....

Cut grass:..

Garlic:..

Wet dogs:...

Ocean:..

Pumpkin pie:..

Cedar: ....

Roses: ....

Cookies baking:..................... ....

Dirt: ....

Bacon:..

Cinnamon:...

Grape:...

Horses:...

Bad Habits Contract

Think about your worst habit, from biting your nails to popping zits. One great way to stop is to write a contract to yourself and decide on a treat you will indulge in once you nix the bad habit.

I, ... ,
(your full name)

agree to quit ....
(bad habit)

as of today, ... The reasons I
(date)

want to stop this bad habit include the following: ....

....
(your reasons for quitting)

When I quit, I will reward myself with ....

.... !
(your reward for quitting)

I know I can do it, because ....

....
(your strengths that will help you quit)

Pamper Yourself!

Part of feeling *pretty* and confident is *pampering yourself,* such as taking a hot bath or getting your toes done at a salon.

What things do you do to relax and treat yourself? ....

....

....

....

....

....

....

....

....

✿ Body Hygiene ....

Crazy Changes ✿

So many parts of your body are changing right now! To keep from getting stressed out and overwhelmed it's helpful to write about things that are changing.

Your teeth are: ....

....

....

Your feet are: ....

....

....

The change that makes you feel grown up: ....

....

....

Body Hygiene ❁

The freakiest body change you've noticed recently: ....

....

The biggest change in your skin: ....

....

....

The thing you're most self-conscious about: ....

....

The thing you hope changes: ....

....

....

The thing you hope doesn't change:

....

....

Puberty

Acne Angst

Ew, zits are the worst. It seems like one day your skin is totally clear and the next day — bam — breakouts! Vent your acne angst here.

Pimples are so ....

I usually break out more often when ....

Waking up with a zit makes me want to ....

I always get them on my ....

The best way to zap a zit is ....

If it won't go away, I ....

Secretly, I wish I had skin like ....

My one skin wish would be ....

....

You Glow Girl!

When you feel great, it shows on your face. As someone once said, "I've never seen a smiling face *that was not beautiful.*" Make a list of *the things that make you happy* and glow. (You'll forget all about that zit on your nose, we promise.)

....

....

....

....

....

....

....

....

....

....

Skin Tips ✿ ✿

Drinking lots of water, keeping your hair off your face, and never picking a pimple are ways to keep your skin fresh and healthy-looking. Jot down some of your favorite tips and products for clear, beautiful skin.

Dermatologist Visit

Have you ever seen a dermatologist about your skin? What advice did he or she give you?

❀ Puberty ....

Your First Period

It finally happened! You got your first period. Describe how you reacted and felt on that crazy day. Who was the first person you told? Did you feel different afterward?

....

....

....

....

....

....

....

....

....

....

PMS

PMS is a lame part of getting your period for most girls. It means feeling pretty weird and icky for a few days before and during your period. Check off the symptoms you have experienced, and then learn to cope with PMS by exercising, staying extra hydrated, getting a good night's sleep, and pampering yourself with things like a bath.

PMS symptoms:

☐ moody

☐ irritable

☐ crying for no reason

☐ super tired

☐ trouble sleeping

☐ cravings, especially for salty or sweet foods

☐ breakouts

☐ sore breasts

☐ cramps

☐ feeling bloated

☐ headaches

☐ constipation or diarrhea

Being Prepared ✳

Don't let your period catch you off-guard. It might not come regularly for awhile, so use the following checklist to be totally prepared!

☐ Buy a box of pads or tampons to keep in the bathroom at home

☐ Buy a box of pantyliners for your light days and to wear to bed

☐ Stash one or two pads or tampons in your locker or backpack for school

☐ Places like restaurants usually have tampon machines, so carry quarters in case you need to buy one while you're on-the-go

☐ Talk to your doctor and your mom about a pain reliever like Advil if you have cramps or get headaches

☐ Get a heating pad for really crampy days

Other ideas:...

....

....

....

....

....

Tampons vs. Pads

Every girl has a different opinion on tampons and pads, and there are pros and cons to both.

For instance, some girls aren't super comfortable inserting a tampon, so they stick to pads. Pads are really easy to use, and pantyliners are great for light periods; however, a thicker pad can feel bulky! Also, you won't be able to go swimming in pads and they may shift around during sports.

On the flip side, tampons definitely take some practice, but they don't make a mess and you can swim and run and jump around. Just go with whatever you're comfortable with!

What's your preference, and why? ....

....

....

....

....

....

....

Keep Track of Your Period

Start keeping track of your period, the start and end dates during each cycle, and how you feel around that time, and you will eventually be able to anticipate when it is coming.

Body changes I notice right before my period: ....

....

....

Mood changes I notice right before my period: ....

....

....

My period usually lasts for about .... days.

My period is the heaviest on day ....

Period Tracker!

1 Start Date: .... End Date:..

2 Start Date: .... End Date:..

3 Start Date: .... End Date:..

4 Start Date: .... End Date:..

5 Start Date: .... End Date:..

6 Start Date: .... End Date:..

7 Start Date: .... End Date:..

8 Start Date: .... End Date:..

9 Start Date: .... End Date:..

10 Start Date: .... End Date:..

11 Start Date: .... End Date:..

12 Start Date: .... End Date:..

Bra Shopping ✻

Talk about getting your first bra.

What kind was it?..

....

....

Who took you to buy it and where did you shop?...

....

....

Were you embarrassed or relieved to be wearing a bra?...

....

....

Did you feel cool or weird?..

....

Best Breast

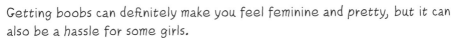

Getting boobs can definitely make you feel feminine and pretty, but it can also be a hassle for some girls.

How do you feel about your boobs?
Are they too small, too big, or just the right size?..

....

The best thing about having boobs:..

....

The worst thing about having boobs:

....

....

....

What would your perfect bra size be?

....

....

Size Wise

Your boobs will probably keep growing and changing shape over the next few years. Use this chart to record your bra size as it changes. And just remember, no matter how voluptuous or small and perky your boobs are, someone is wishing she looked like you!

Date:... Notes:...

....

Age:... ....

Bra Size:... ....

Date:... Notes:...

....

Age:... ....

Bra Size:... ....

Date: ....

Age: ....

Bra Size: ....

Notes: ....

....

....

Date: ....

Age: ....

Bra Size: ....

Notes: ....

....

....

Date: ....

Age: ....

Bra Size: ....

Notes: ....

....

....

Did you know that more than 70 percent of women wear the wrong bra size? If your bra creeps up in the back, gaps in the cups, or if the straps leave grooves in your shoulders, you are wearing the wrong bra style or size. To get the perfect fit, visit a specialty store and have a salesperson measure you — she can do this right over your clothes.

Shaving!

The first time you shave is always a little comical. Maybe you stole your dad's razor and ended up cutting your knee 20 times. Write about the first time you shaved.

....

....

....

....

....

....

....

....

....

....

....

Hair Where?

Everyone has hair in weird places, like on their toes or below their belly button. It stinks, but all girls have the same problem, so you're not alone. What hair do you absolutely hate? Do you plan to remove it or cover it?

❀ Puberty ....

OMG!

Puberty and periods and body changes make for some seriously embarrassing moments. What is your most OMG moment?

....

....

....

....

....

....

Rate Your OMG Moment:

☐ Bright red in the face
(☆ ☆)

☐ People will be talking
for a week
(☆ ☆ ☆)

☐ Total humiliation. Like,
I wanted to switch schools
(☆ ☆ ☆ ☆)

Your Weight

Everyone knows weight is a *hot topic* for girls, and, realistically, *most girls* will gain weight during *puberty.*

How do you feel about
your weight right now? ....

....

....

....

....

Are you *happy* and comfortable with what you weigh? ....

....

....

....

....

What healthy things do you do to maintain a good weight? ....

....

....

....

....

Health Issues

Favorite Foods

What is your favorite restaurant? ....

....

What food could you eat every single day? ....

What is your favorite meal that your mom or dad cooks for you? ....

....

If you had to request a last meal, what would you choose? ....

....

What is your guilty food pleasure? ....

If you could make one food fat and calorie-free, what would you choose?

....

Personal Food Pyramid

So, we all know we're supposed to eat a certain number of servings from each of the 6 food groups to get a balanced diet. List your favorite healthy foods in each category to help you plan meals and eat well!

Fats, Oils & Sweets: ....

....

Dairy: ....

....

Meat, Fish, Beans, Eggs & Nuts: ....

....

Veggies: ....

....

Fruits: ....

....

Breads, Rice & Pasta: ....

....

....

Eat This, Not That

Some meals and snacks are total energy zappers (ever been in a Food Coma?) and some will fill you up and give you energy for your whole day. Make a list of the unhealthy meals and snacks you like and then come up with some healthier alternatives.

Eat This:

Not That:

Emotional Eating?

You're going through a lot right now — everything is changing with your body, your friends, your feelings and more. Just be wary of something called "emotional eating" — eating out of loneliness, boredom, anger, stress, or being tired. You might have a bad day at school or go through a tough breakup and turn to food for comfort. Also, some people reward themselves with food; however, a celebration should not mean eating an entire pizza!

Here are some non-food related ways to cheer up, relieve stress, or celebrate:

- Exercise
- Go shopping
- Call a friend
- Listen to music

Come up with a few of your own!

....

....

....

....

....

....

Early to Bed, Early to Rise

Kids our age underestimate how important it is to get a good night's sleep! You need *plenty of rest* to get through your day; plus, people who don't get enough sleep are more likely to get sick or be overweight.

What time do you go to bed on school nights?...

On weekends?...

When do you wake up during the week?..

On weekends?...

When you don't get enough sleep, how do you feel?.....................................

....

What do you do when you need an energy boost?...

....

Sleep Science

If you find it tough to fall asleep at night, it might be related to the changes your body is going through. Something called circadian rhythm — basically, your internal clock — changes during puberty. Plus, you're dealing with boys, grades, friends, family, and other stuff that can keep you up at night.

Here are some good tips for falling asleep faster; check off the ones that work for you!

☐ Don't exercise within an hour before bed

☐ Avoid caffeine or energy drinks after 5 p.m.

☐ Turn off the TV and computer at least 30 minutes before bed

☐ Write down a list of things that are on your mind, then trust yourself to deal with them the next day

☐ Make sure your bed is comfortable and the temperature in your room is stable

☐ Read for 15 minutes in bed to help you relax

☐ Avoid having a large meal right before bedtime

☐ Take a bath before bed to relax

☐ Stick to a regular sleep schedule. Even on the weekends!

Safe Sun Survey

Take our Safe Sun Survey:
Each *"Yes"* answer is worth
either 1 or 0 points.

- Do you wear lotion with SPF 15 or higher on your face every day? **(1 point)**

- Do you go to tanning beds? **(0 points)**

- Do you agree that having a *"base tan"* keeps you from burning? **(0 points)**

- Do you use self-tanners or spray tanning? **(1 point)**

- Do you to get sunburned at least once in the summer? **(0 points)**

- Do you skip sunscreen if it's cloudy? **(0 points)**

- Do you own a chapstick or lipgloss with SPF to protect your lips? **(1 point)**

- Do you pack a bottle of sunscreen in your bag if you're going to a baseball game or the beach? **(1 point)**

- Do you put on more sunscreen after swimming or playing a sport? **(1 point)**

0 to 2 points: You're not doing enough to protect your body and face from sun damage! You should be wearing a face lotion with a minimum of SPF 15 every day, and don't forget about areas like the part in your hair, your lips, the tops of your feet, etc. If you want a golden glow, consider sunless tanning instead.

3 to 5 points: You're practicing good safe sun, which means you'll have fewer wrinkles and dark spots when you're older — and hello, reduced risk of skin cancer! Keep an extra bottle of sunscreen in your beach bag or locker and help your girlfriends out, too!

Soothing Scoliosis

Scoliosis really stinks, but there are some activities that can help. (You should check 'em out even if you don't have back problems!)

The first is **yoga**, which can help your spine's alignment and strengthen back muscles. And yoga can definitely improve your posture.

The second is **swimming**, which is great because your body weight is supported by the water, so there isn't much pain or strain on your spine. Plus, swimming is a great aerobic workout!

Try out yoga and swimming, then write about your experience. Did they help with pain? Did you enjoy your workout?

Sports & Fitness

Fitness Fanatic

How often do you exercise? ....

What is your favorite form of exercise? ....

What is a kind of exercise you hate? ....

Do you like to work out with any friends? ....

What sports do you play? ....

If you could be a world-class athlete in any sport, which would it be?...........

....

How do you feel after you work out or play a sport?...

....

What is your greatest moment of athletic glory? ....

....

Who is your favorite sports star of all time?...

....

No More Excuses!

It's easy to make excuses for not exercising, like "I'm too tired," or "I don't have enough time." But now is the best time to get in healthy habits — it'll only get tougher from here! Write down your biggest obstacles to exercise, then jot down a way to overcome each excuse.

An example:

Excuse: I don't have enough time.

Solution: Use half of my lunch break to go for a walk

Excuse: ....

Solution: ....

Excuse: ....

Solution: ....

Excuse: ....

Solution: ....

Excuse: ....

Solution: ....

Excuse: ....

Solution: ....

Move Your Body!

Exercise is awesome, and many times, you don't even need a gym. Put a check mark next to the activities you enjoy or could take up. There might be a few you hadn't even considered!

☐ Frisbee

☐ Walking the dog

☐ Running

☐ Tossing the football

☐ Bike ride

☐ Hiking

☐ Kayaking

☐ Tennis

☐ Ice skating

☐ Rollerblading

☐ Swimming

☐ Rock climbing

☐ Sledding

☐ Trampoline

☐ Skateboard

☐ Surfing

☐ Yoga

☐ Dancing

☐ Climbing a tree

☐ Ballet

☐ Gardening

☐ Golfing

☐ Horseback riding

☐ Playing Tag

☐ Vacuuming

☐ Mowing the lawn

☐ Push-ups

☐ Jumping rope

☐ Bowling

☐ Shopping

Place a *photo of you doing your*
favorite outdoor activity
or sport here.

Write about your favorite outdoor activity or sport and why you enjoy it.

....

....

....

Workout Calendar

People say it takes about 30 days for something to become a habit. Use this one-month calendar to record the days you exercise, what you do, and how you feel. You'll start noticing that just a few days of moderate exercise every week are enough to help you have more energy, feel great, and even slim down.

Month:..

Results:

Number of days I
worked out this month:..............

I feel ... .

....

....

....

....

MON.	TUES.
exercise:	exercise:
mood:	mood:
exercise:	exercise:
mood:	mood:
exercise:	exercise:
mood:	mood:
exercise:	exercise:
mood:	mood:
exercise:	exercise:
mood:	mood:

WED.	THURS.	FRI.	SAT.	SUN.
exercise:	exercise:	exercise:	exercise:	exercise:
mood:	mood:	mood:	mood:	mood:
exercise:	exercise:	exercise:	exercise:	exercise:
mood:	mood:	mood:	mood:	mood:
exercise:	exercise:	exercise:	exercise:	exercise:
mood:	mood:	mood:	mood:	mood:
exercise:	exercise:	exercise:	exercise:	exercise:
mood:	mood:	mood:	mood:	mood:
exercise:	exercise:	exercise:	exercise:	exercise:
mood:	mood:	mood:	mood:	mood:

Get Motivated

What motivates you to exercise and eat right? Go over our list, then add your own motivators!

❀ ❀

Swimsuit season!
....

More energy in the morning
....

A big dance
....

Running a 5k
....

Making the varsity team
....

Staying healthy during flu season
....

....

....

....

....

Fitness Test

How many consecutive *push-ups* can you do? How many *sit-ups* can you do in a minute? Test yourself and see how you measure up against the national averages for your age group. If you don't quite measure up, practice for a few weeks and try again. Sit-ups and push-ups are easy and effective ways to build strength.

	AGES 10-12	AGES 13-15	AGES 16-17
Sit-ups (in one minute)	30-35	36-37	34-35
Push-ups	10-13	11-15	12-16

Date:	Sit-ups:	Push-ups:

Emotional Issues ✳ ✳

Freaking Out!

We all have occasional freak outs — I mean, being a girl can be stressful. It can help to vent about the things that are stressing you out on paper, so let loose!

The thing that stresses you out most about your ...

Family:...

Friends: ....

School: ....

Interests:..

Boys:...

Body:...

De-Stress & Decompress

What ways do you deal with stress?
Check off the ways you decompress,
then add your own.

- ☐ Play with your dog
- ☐ Listen to music
- ☐ Go for a run
- ☐ Bake cookies
- ☐ Paint your nails
- ☐ Write a poem

....

....

....

....

....

....

❁ Emotional Issues..

Your Many Moods

We're all aware *that our* moods can change *from* one second *to* the next.
Write down *the* last time you felt these emotions:

Amazed:..

Irritated:...

Scared:..

Anxious:..

Guilty:...

Lonely:..

Bored:...

Blissful:...

Jealous:...

Hopeful:..

.... Emotional Issues ✿

Embarrassed: ....

Creative: ....

Nostalgic: ....

Depressed: ....

Paranoid: ....

Surprised: ....

Cheerful: ....

Respected: ....

Satisfied: ....

Confused: ....

Beautiful: ....

Mischievous: ....

Inspired: ....

Quiz: Optimist, Pessimist, or Realist?

Attitude is everything when you're a teenager! Take this quiz to find out how you view the world and its ups and downs.

1 You get dumped on your birthday. What do you think?
  a. "Oh well, now I can flirt with that cute guy in my art class."
  b. "I'll never meet anyone as cute, smart, or funny. I need a gallon of ice cream."
  c. "What kind of jerk dumps someone on their birthday? He's obviously not the right guy for me. I'll meet someone better."

2 You find out you didn't make the volleyball team. You think:
  a. "Now I'll have more time to hang out with my friends."
  b. "I suck. I'm too embarrassed to face my friends."
  c. "I trained really hard, but it didn't work out. I can try out again next year."

3 You come down with the flu the night before a friend's party. Your first thought is:
  a. "If I rest up I can still make an appearance."
  b. "Of course this would happen right now. My friend is going to hate me."
  c. "Bad timing. I'll send her a birthday present to make up for it."

4 Your best friend is spending the summer in Florida, and you're stuck at home. You think:
  a. "She's so lucky. I can't wait to hear all about it!"
  b. "I never get to do anything fun! My life is so boring."
  c. "I should round up some friends for a road-trip this summer."

5 You are offered a solo in the school play. Your first thought is:

   a. "Hooray!"

   b. "Oh my gosh, I will probably screw up in front of the whole school."

   c. "I'm going to have to practice a lot, but this is a good opportunity."

Mostly a's, Optimist: You maintain a sunny, positive outlook on life, no matter what bumps happen along the way. You might get knocked for being naïve, but people appreciate your ability to see the good in all situations.

Mostly b's, Pessimist: When things go wrong, you often blame yourself, even if it's not your fault. Try and remember that tomorrow is another day, so live and learn. And expect the best — life may surprise you!

Mostly c's, Realist: You tell it like it is. You make the most of good opportunities that come your way and don't get hung up on things you can't control. You know that life has ups and downs, and you're ready to weather them both.

Gratitude List

Loneliness, sadness and even depression can affect anyone. However, one of the best ways to ward off these dark feelings is to be thankful for all the wonderful things in your life (and everyone has them!). From a new flavor of ice cream you liked to a special friend, jot down the big and small things you are grateful for.

....

....

....

....

....

....

....

....

Caring Confidante

If you are feeling really down, it's important to have a confidante — or someone you can talk to who will listen. Whether it's a family member, friend, coach, or teacher, make a list of the people you can confide in when you have a rough day.

When I'm sad about..,

.... is a good shoulder to cry on.

When I'm lonely, I turn to..

When I'm nervous about..,

I can talk to..

When I'm scared about..,

I trust..

When I need love advice, I can talk to..

Quiz: Food Attitude

Every girl stresses about her weight from time to time, but do you have healthy attitudes about food? Take our quiz and find out.

1 You ate a bag of chips with lunch. You:

  a. Enjoy every single bite when you treat yourself

  b. Feel guilty all day

  c. Get another for an afternoon snack, too!

2 You get invited to a pool party, so you:

  a. Try to eat more fruits and veggies until then

  b. Eat nothing but lettuce for the next two weeks

  c. Pick out a new swimsuit, then go for pizza

3 Your crush gets a girlfriend, and you're brokenhearted. You:

  a. Go for a run to blow off some steam

  b. Eat a whole pint of ice cream and feel totally sick

  c. Eat a bowl of ice cream — you deserve it after your bad day

4 You're trying to cut back on sweets, but a friend brings in birthday cake. When you're offered a piece, you:

a. Ask for a small piece and don't worry about finishing the whole thing

b. Say, "Oh gosh, sorry, I can't, I'm on a diet."

c. Grab a piece and come back for seconds. Yum.

5 You order spaghetti at a restaurant and a humongous plate is set down in front of you. You:

a. Eat half, then take the rest home as leftovers

b. Look down and you've eaten the whole thing — what happened?

c. Order garlic bread and dessert too!

Mostly a's: Congrats, you have a healthy attitude about food! You eat less-healthy foods only in moderation and exercise good willpower. You don't forget that eating is fun and that the occasional treat is nothing to stress about!

Mostly b's: Food freaks you out, causing you to overeat or not eat enough at times. There's no need to worry so much about every bite that you eat, as long as you get moderate exercise a few days a week and treat yourself every once in a while.

Mostly c's: While there's no need to deprive yourself, you can't indulge in sweets and junk every time you feel like it! Also remember that food is fuel, not a reward after a tough day. It's important to get into healthy eating habits now so you have lots of energy, and so you don't become a junk-food junkie and pack on the pounds down the road.

Friends & Self-Esteem

It's Great Being You!

Maybe you felt awesome when you got an A in Math, or you felt really cute in your new boots last week. No matter what gives you confidence or pride, make a list here for the days when you need a little pick-me-up.

I feel *proud* when: ....

I feel *smart* when: ....

I feel *pretty* when: ....

I feel *most confident* when: ....

I feel *popular* when: ....

I feel *most comfortable* when: ....

I feel *most loved* when: ....

Let's Rewind

Figuring out life and getting comfortable in your own skin takes awhile and will have a few learning experiences along the way. It's OK to need a "takeback" from time to time, as long as you learn something from the mistake and move forward. Describe a time when you wished you could rewind and change something you did.

....

....

....

....

....

....

....

....

....

World's Greatest Friends

Write your closest friends' names and what you love about them or what makes them special to you.

name: ....
comments: ....
....

name: ....
comments: ....
....

My BFF!

name: ....

  comments: ....
....

name: ....
comments: ....
....

name: ....
comments: ....
....

name: ....
comments: ....
....

name: ....
comments: ....
....

name: ....
comments: ....
....

Stand Your Ground

Describe a situation when you were *tempted* or *pressured* to do something you didn't feel comfortable with or didn't agree with. Talk about what happened, how you avoided the tricky situation, and how you felt afterward.

Expert Advice

Do your friends tell you that you give great advice? Are you the Dear Abby of your basketball team? Now's your chance to show what you know and be the friendship and dating expert by answering these girls' questions.

To Spin or Not to Spin: I went to a guy-girl party a few weeks ago and they wanted to play Spin the Bottle, where you have to kiss whoever the bottle points to. I felt really awkward, so I left the room, but at school on Monday everyone was calling me a baby. What should I do next time? Should I just play? ~ From Kendra

....

....

....

....

....

....

Longtime Friend Dilemna: I have a friend from when I was little who is kind of a dork. When I was having lunch with my popular friends, she walked by and said hi. I totally ignored her! Now I feel bad, but I don't want my new friends to think I'm lame. What should I do? ~ From Steph

❀ Friends & Self-Esteem ....

Friend or Frenemy? Even *though* I study way *more,* my best friend always does better on our *history tests* than me. I just want to scream when we compare grades. Why do I get so jealous and mad, and how can I stop? It's starting to interfere with our friendship. I mean, she's my best friend, so why do I care so much? ~ From Emma

Do I Date Him? I have a huge problem — my friend has had a crush on this guy for forever, but he recently told me that he wants to hang out with me! If I say yes, I'm afraid my friend will be mad. And I don't want to say no, because he's one of the hottest guys in our school. What should I do? ~ From Lindsey

Genie in a Bottle

Poof! A genie suddenly appears and grants you three wishes!
What do you wish for?

1

I wish for ...

2

I wish for ...

3

I wish for ...

Hopes & Dreams

My goal for the upcoming year:...

....

A friend I know will always be in my life:...

A skill I'd like to develop: ....

A fortune I'd like to find in my fortune cookie:...

....

Where would I like to be living in 5 years, and why? ....

....

My dream job would be:..

I want .... kids; .... boys and .... girls.

Names I like for kids:...

One person I would like to meet, and why? ....

....

One thing I want to do in my lifetime:...

....

I always want my friends and family to remember me as:.................................

....

A Letter to Yourself

Write a letter to your future self. Write about your goals and dreams and the greatest things about being a teenager.

Other books by:

Isabel & Emily Lluch

The Ultimate Girls' Guide
To Understanding and Caring for Your Body

Comprehensive, Fun, and Easy to Read!

By Isabel & Emily Lluch
• age 16 •　　• age 13 •
Answering questions from girls just like you!

Plus valuable tips and advice from a panel of experts

Filled with important information all growing girls must know.

US $12.95/paperback; ISBN-13: 978-1-934386-43-9; Size: 7" x 11", 132pp

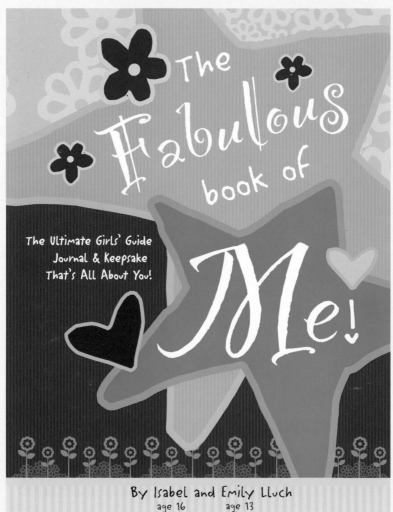

The Fabulous book of Me!

The Ultimate Girls' Guide
Journal & Keepsake
That's All About You!

By Isabel and Emily Lluch
age 16   age 13

A one-of-a-kind keepsake that's all about you!

US $16.95/hardcover; ISBN-13: 978-1-934386-57-6; Size: 6" x 8.75", 100pp